How Ships Are Made

Text David A. Thomas
Design Eddie Poulton

Contents

Facts On File
New York • Oxford

All Kinds of Ships

If you took a trip around one of the great harbors of the world – San Francisco, or Hong Kong, or Sydney for example – no matter what the time of day or night, you would be amazed at the variety of ships to be seen. Alongside the wharves, lying at anchor or plying their way across the open sea, would be ships of all shapes and sizes: tankers and cargo vessels, liners and container ships, frigates and ferries. The figure might run into the hundreds, because the needs of commerce and trade throughout the world are so diverse.

If the cargo to be transported is liquid – such as oil – the ship will look very much like a huge floating tank (hence "tanker"). Nowadays many cargoes are fitted into standard-sized boxes, or containers, which are packed solid with goods and stacked into the holds and on the decks of ships. The container system, as well as being compact, also makes for easy handling by cranes, from ship to truck or from truck to ship.

In general it is cheaper to transport bulk cargoes such as oil and chemicals in larger vessels, so modern designers have produced bigger and better ships known as Very Large and Ultra Large Crude Carriers – or VLCC and ULCC for short; the name crude simply defines the cargoes of oil or chemicals, often referred to as ores.

In order to carry oil one way and ores on the return voyage – thus avoiding the costly waste of a ship returning empty – OBO (Oil/Bulk/Ore) carriers have been developed.

In spite of all the many complexities, ships can be grouped into four basic categories:

COMMERCIAL TRANSPORTERS This is the largest and most important commercial category. As well as the massive bulk carriers of oil and ores and other products, this group also includes refrigerated ships (known as "Reefers"), liquified petroleum and natural gas ships, general cargo vessels of every description, and a large variety of container ships.

Some vessels – for example ferries and Roll-On-Roll-Off ("Ro-Ro") ships – carry passengers as well as goods, thus overlapping with:

PASSENGER CARRIERS Included in this group are many types of ship, from luxury liners to river- and channel-crossing ferries used by tens of millions of people throughout the world.

SPECIAL DUTY SHIPS This includes a variety of ships designed to carry out special tasks in all sorts of conditions, from polar seas to tropical waters. Their duties include cable-laying, oil-drilling, dredging, trawling for fish, and scientific work such as oceanography and seismic surveys. They vary in size from a whaling factory ship to a **dredger**, from a floating crane to a Mississippi barge or a LASH (Lighter Aboard Ship) vessel. They can be of the very simplest design and construction or as complex and sophisticated as a satellite tracking ship.

Left. Two tankers anchored offshore in the Persian Gulf. The one on the left is "light" (empty); the one on the right is fully loaded. Tankers load and unload their cargoes at specially constructed fueling jetties, from which the oil is transferred by means of pumps.

Cruise liners operate in Scandinavian, Mediterranean, West Indian and Far Eastern waters. Emphasis is on luxury passenger accommodation, lounges, swimming pools, restaurants and sports decks.

Countries such as Canada, Finland and the USSR operate fleets of icebreakers to keep their harbors and rivers open in winter. The breakers have specially reinforced bows that ride up onto the floes and crush their way through them. Their propellers are shielded from the floating ice. The picture shows the Russian breaker *Ormov* at work.

The *Yuri Gagarin,* a Russian satellite tracking ship which is also used for investigating conditions in the upper atmosphere and that can monitor and control spacecraft. At 45,000 tons, she is Russia's largest research vessel.

Warships

The design of warships, like that of commercial vessels, is determined by the jobs that they have to do. The complicated weaponry systems employed today, and the special roles of warships, provide designers and builders with challenges that they do not encounter in commercial shipbuilding.

Most of the world's modern warships can be classified as follows:

AIRCRAFT CARRIERS These are the largest and most powerful warships. The US Navy's *Nimitz* **class**, weighing over 90,000 tons, carries more than 5,000 men and nearly 100 aircraft: jet fighters armed with conventional weapons, guided missiles or nuclear warheads, and helicopters used for detecting, locating and destroying submarines. Carriers are, in fact, mobile, floating airfields of strategic importance that can move rapidly to the trouble spots of the world. All these special requirements have to be taken into consideration by the naval architect and his design team.

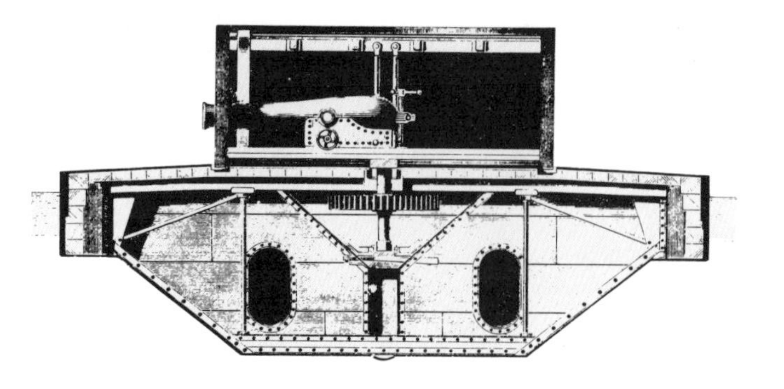

A cross-section of the American Federal ship *Monitor*, showing her revolving gun turret machinery. The ironclad *Monitor* fought a famous sea duel with the Confederate vessel *Virginia*, but her lack of buoyancy made her unsafe at sea and she foundered in 1862 within a year of launching.

SUBMARINES The American and British navies classify this type of warship into the following three groups:

- SSBN Nuclear Powered and Ballistic Missile Armed
- SSN Nuclear Powered, Fleet Type
- SS Conventional Diesel/Electric for Patrol Duties

Above. The US Navy's nuclear submarine *Los Angeles* is classified SSN and unlike the SSBNs does not carry ballistic missiles. But she is a formidable vessel: she has a displacement of nearly 7,000 tons submerged, a speed of more than 30 knots and is armed with guided missiles.

Left. Of the few battleships left in the world today, the USS *Iowa* is one of the largest, with a full load displacement of 58,000 tons. She is shown here demonstrating the massive power of her nine 16-inch (406 mm) guns.

Right. The angled flight deck and steam-powered catapult, both British inventions, are among the new design features of the recently modernized French aircraft carrier *Foch*, which also bristles with radar and communications antennae.

Because it has to balance a number of conflicting needs, this is perhaps the most complex class of vessel. For example, high speed is desirable while submerged, but it must be accompanied by very low noise levels – and these two qualities do not go well together. A submarine must be able to submerge to great depths and pressures but these must not adversely affect the sensitivity of **sensors** and weapons.

A submarine (which is called a boat, not a ship) has to carry, to fire and to control a mix of underwater and above-water weapons, and at the same time has to avoid detection by **sonar** equipment – and to survive attacks by anti-submarine explosives. These are problems that the naval architect has to overcome.

CRUISERS, DESTROYERS AND FRIGATES All these surface ships are similar in shape and function, but they vary considerably in size: from about 2,000 tons for the smallest frigate to about 15,000 tons for a modern guided-missile cruiser. The US Navy – the largest in the world – has about thirty-six cruisers in commission.

The destroyer's role is to provide anti-submarine and air defense for a group of ships in a hostile environment. She is a long, graceful ship capable of high speeds. Her missiles and guns allow her to engage air and surface targets, and she is also specially equipped for anti-submarine warfare.

The frigate also has an anti-aircraft and anti-submarine role, with skilled technicians to operate her computer-assisted sonar and communications systems. The operational role of a frigate is similar to that of a destroyer.

MINOR AND AUXILIARY VESSELS Scores of other types of ship are built for naval service, with requirements as varied as those for commercial vessels. They include minesweepers; a range of amphibious vessels that carry army personnel, tanks, etc; oilers and repair ships; cutters for the US Coast Guard Service.

At the battle of the Armada in 1588, it was the speed and maneuverability of the English ships that helped them to outsail the Spanish fleet.

History

Shipbuilding is among the most ancient of crafts, possibly originating in its simplest form by ancient man watching a floating tree trunk. The oldest ship ever discovered is the oared funeral ship of the Egyptian Pharaoh Cheops (3969 – 3908 BC).

Centuries later the Romans were building great fighting **galleys** of pine and cedar, with oars arranged in banks up to five tiers high.

When Roman influence declined, Norsemen constructed stout, seaworthy vessels, some of which sailed the Atlantic.

Henry VIII built a fine 1,000 ton ship named *Henri Grâce à Dieu*, 138 feet (47 meters) long, but Phineas Pett built an even more splendid ship for King Charles I, the fabulous *Sovereign of the Seas*, a three-decker of 1,637 tons (the same figure as the year in which she was launched). The Pett family produced no fewer than ten master shipwrights between the years 1550 to 1660. Phineas was the first president of the Shipwright's Company, in 1612, and it was he who introduced the first frigate in the 17th century.

By the early 19th century British ascendancy in shipbuilding was beginning to be challenged by the Americans, whose rival endeavors to win the Eastern tea trade resulted in the construction of the famous tea **clippers**.

But it was the coming of the steam engine that revolutionized the shipbuilding industry. It produced the great Victorian paddle-driven and the later, more efficient, screw-propelled steamers, the first of which was Isambard Kingdom Brunel's magnificent *Great Britain*. Weighing 3,936 tons, she was 322 feet (98.1 meters) long, and in 1845 she crossed the Atlantic from Liverpool, England, to New York in a record-breaking 14½ days. Brunel was one of the world's greatest engineers who designed and built ships, tunnels, bridges and railways, inspired by ideas which were years ahead of his time.

At the beginning of the 20th century the steam engine was quickly followed by the **turbine engine** and this improvement was adopted for passenger steamers – especially on the transatlantic service. Shipbuilding entered the era of giant passenger liners, which in turn has given way to cruise ships offering passengers every kind of luxury.

In recent times nuclear power has emerged as a means of propulsion, but the immense cost of installation and the need for shielding the crew from radiation restricts its use to naval vessels, particularly to submarines.

Warships, too, benefited from the developments in design and technology. However, in England it took a tug-of-war between the screw-propelled sloop *Rattler* and the paddle-driven *Alecto* before the Admiralty would admit the superiority of screw propulsion.

Improved guns and projectiles hastened the use of iron **cladding** for ship protection, and gradually the transition to all-metal ships was made. In 1860 the first frigate (subsequently rated a battleship) to be constructed entirely of iron was built on the River Thames. She was HMS *Warrior*, weighing 9,210 tons.

During the American Civil War each side was equipped with iron-clad vessels, the most innovative being the Federal *Monitor*. Mounted on her deck was a revolving gun turret made of iron 8 inches thick. But her hull was only a few inches above the waterline, making her unseaworthy, and in 1862 she foundered.

In 1906 the battleship HMS *Dreadnought* was launched. She had been built in one year and a day – an incredible feat of engineering. Weighing 17,900 tons, with ten 12-inch guns in five turrets, she was the first "all-big-gun" battleship. She was also the first to be driven by turbines, which gave her a speed of 21 **knots**. She made all other battleships obsolete.

In the mid-20th century, far-reaching advances in maritime and aviation sciences have enabled naval architects to develop completely new concepts in the design of warships. These ideas have been applied particularly to aircraft carriers and SSBN submarines.

The famous clippers, which originated in Baltimore, represented the high point of sailing-ship design. (Right) The record-breaking *Cutty Sark* is now preserved at Greenwich in England.

Below. The *Great Eastern,* designed by I.K. Brunel, under construction. When launched in 1858 she was more than three times the size of the largest ship in the world.

Shipyard Administration

In the early 1940s, during World War II, a great many British merchant ships were being sunk by German **U-boats**, and it was impossible to replace them quickly enough. To the rescue came Henry Kaiser, an American, whose shipyard on the Pacific coast of the US had the astonishing capacity to construct vessels of about 10,500 tons in no more than ten days. Known as *Liberty ships*, they attained a speed of 11 knots. In all, 2,270 were built.

Kaiser's success lay in his ingenious and revolutionary methods of administration – which were so efficient that they are still applied in the best shipyards today.

In the building of a ship, the first essential is to ensure that the whole operation is meticulously planned, so that production – the actual manufacturing process – can run smoothly. Carrying out this work are teams of people who are skilled both in administration and in the various shipbuilding trades and crafts. They can be grouped as follows:

MARKETING AND SALES MANAGER Under his supervision, estimates of the cost of a new ship are prepared, market trends are studied, and promotional material – such as brochures and leaflets and manuals – is produced.

CHIEF NAVAL ARCHITECT His responsibility is to ensure that the ship he designs is seaworthy and that it meets the operational requirements of the owner. He supervises a large and important department of specialist designers, draftsmen, and computer operators.

TECHNICAL MANAGER From the information provided by the Chief Naval Architect, the Technical Manager is responsible for producing meticulously accurate drawings for the Production Manager. He and his department are also involved in providing drawings and technical information for the outside contractors who supply machinery and equipment for fitting.

PRODUCTION MANAGER He leads a large team responsible for the actual construction of a ship. His aim is to produce it on time and according to the specifications. He is also responsible for organizing the launch of the ship.

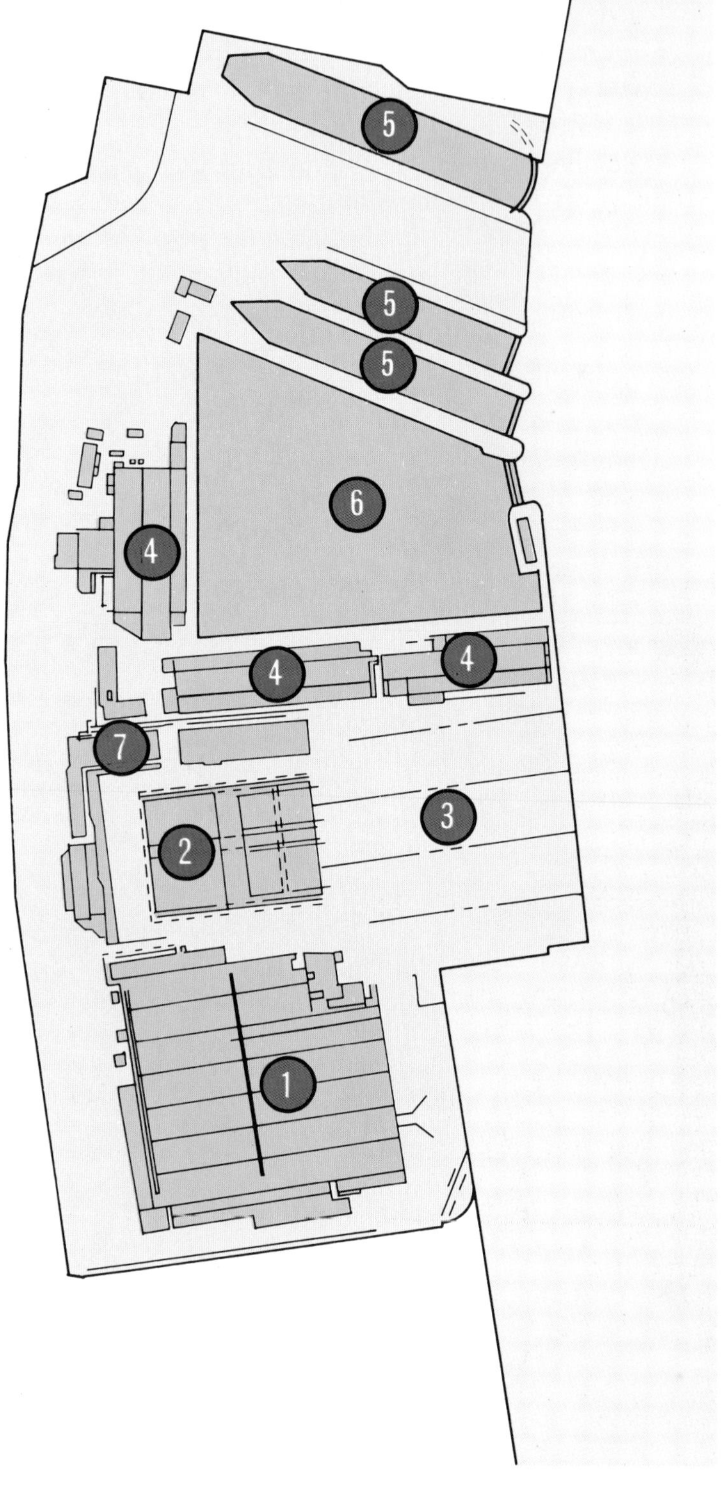

This construction site at a modern shipyard (No. 2 on the plan above) is like a vast sports arena, big enough to accommodate two dozen tennis courts. The 14.4-acre assemblage area (6) is larger than ten full-size football fields.

1. Steel fabrication shops.
2. Construction Hall, showing two building berths.
3. Slipways — ships are extruded from the Hall and then launched into the river or harbor.
4. Outfit production shops, where much of the pre-outfitting work is done.
5. Dry docks. Three are provided for new construction work and for ships needing repairs.
6. Non-tidal Fitting-out basin — an inner harbor where work on the ship is completed before acceptance sea trials.
7. Administrative offices.

ENGINEERS There are a variety of engineering departments, each headed by a specialist. For example, the Quality Control Engineer is in charge of the Inspection Department, which ensures that all manufactured parts meet required standards; the Plant Engineer supervises the efficient maintenance of the yard's own plant and equipment.

COMPUTER PROGRAMMERS Their work helps to simplify the manufacturing process through the use of computers at all stages: administration, design, planning and construction.

SUPPORT FUNCTION PERSONNEL These are office staff who are responsible for secretarial, legal, purchasing and stock control and who work closely with accounts and financial control staff.

CRAFT TRADES WORKERS These can be broadly divided into the following two categories:

Shipbuilding	*Fitting Out*
Welders	Electricians
Drillers & Riveters	Pipefitters & Welders
Blacksmiths	Sheet Metal Workers
Platers	Woodworkers
Shipwrights (Joiners)	Painters

As well as the thousands of workers employed in the shipyard, a large number of contractors outside the yard are used: such as engine, radio, radar and electrical manufacturers.

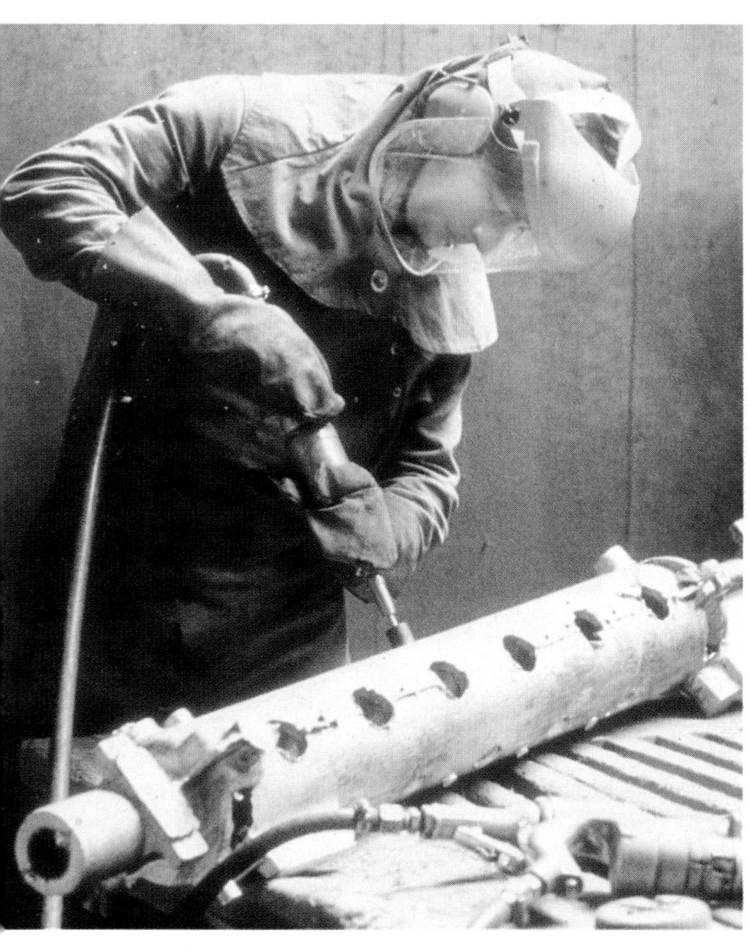

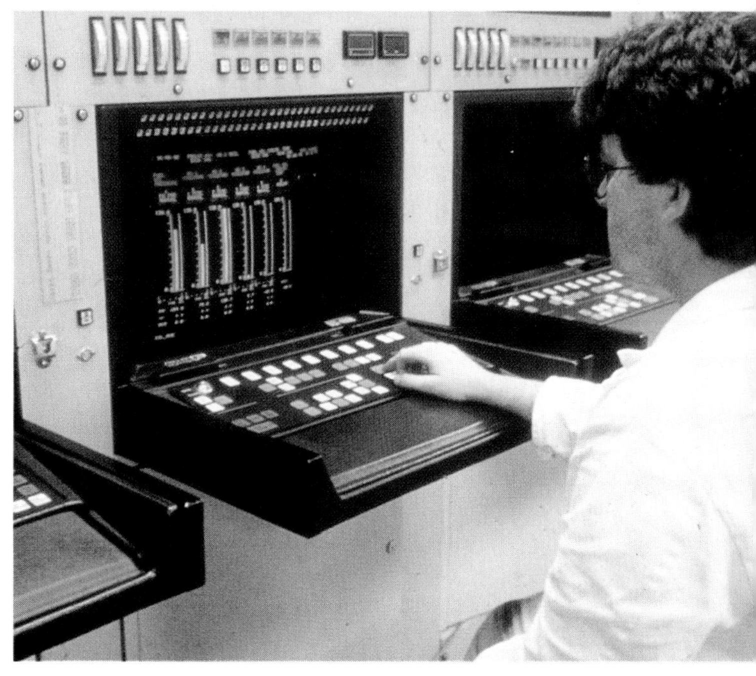

Above. A craftsman wears protective clothing while working on a casting block.

Right, above. Engineered components must be machined to fine tolerances. An inspector checks for accuracy. (Below) Modern technology in shipbuilding has created a demand for highly trained and technically competent operators.

An operator works at a section of a computer system used in ship design. The picture shows the zoom-in facility that assists in checking a complicated diagram.

Right. A design-computer screen showing the general layout of a merchant ship in plan as well as in profile. (Inset) The operator can select individual compartments from the plan and enlarge them in order to check details.

Computer Assisted Design

The design of ships has been revolutionized by the digital computer. In the past, much of the naval architect's work consisted of monotonous, time-consuming mathematical calculations. His team of designers would spend many days determining a ship's stability, her strengths, and her motions in the unpredictable wave formations of a seaway.

Today, analysis by Computer Assisted Design and Manufacture – **CAD/CAM** for short – has changed the actual design work of ships structures. It has opened up whole new possibilities for designers, allowing them not only to speed up their day-to-day work, but offering them design features never before possible.

The greater part of ship design – most of the dimensioning – the **scantlings** and shapes of the plating and other structural steel work – is based on mathematics. It is even used to ensure that the hull shape is faired (made smooth).

So sophisticated is the process, that the computer can predict the ship's behavior well in advance of construction. But in spite of this advanced technology the naval architect still has to undertake his own detailed research to establish his basic data. For example, the requirements of the shipowner will be specified in a document stating the type of the ship that he wants, what her cargo will be, how much she will carry, what propulsion she should have, and even the number of crewmen.

The service and general climatic conditions under which the ship will operate will be noted, as well as any special requirements or limitations

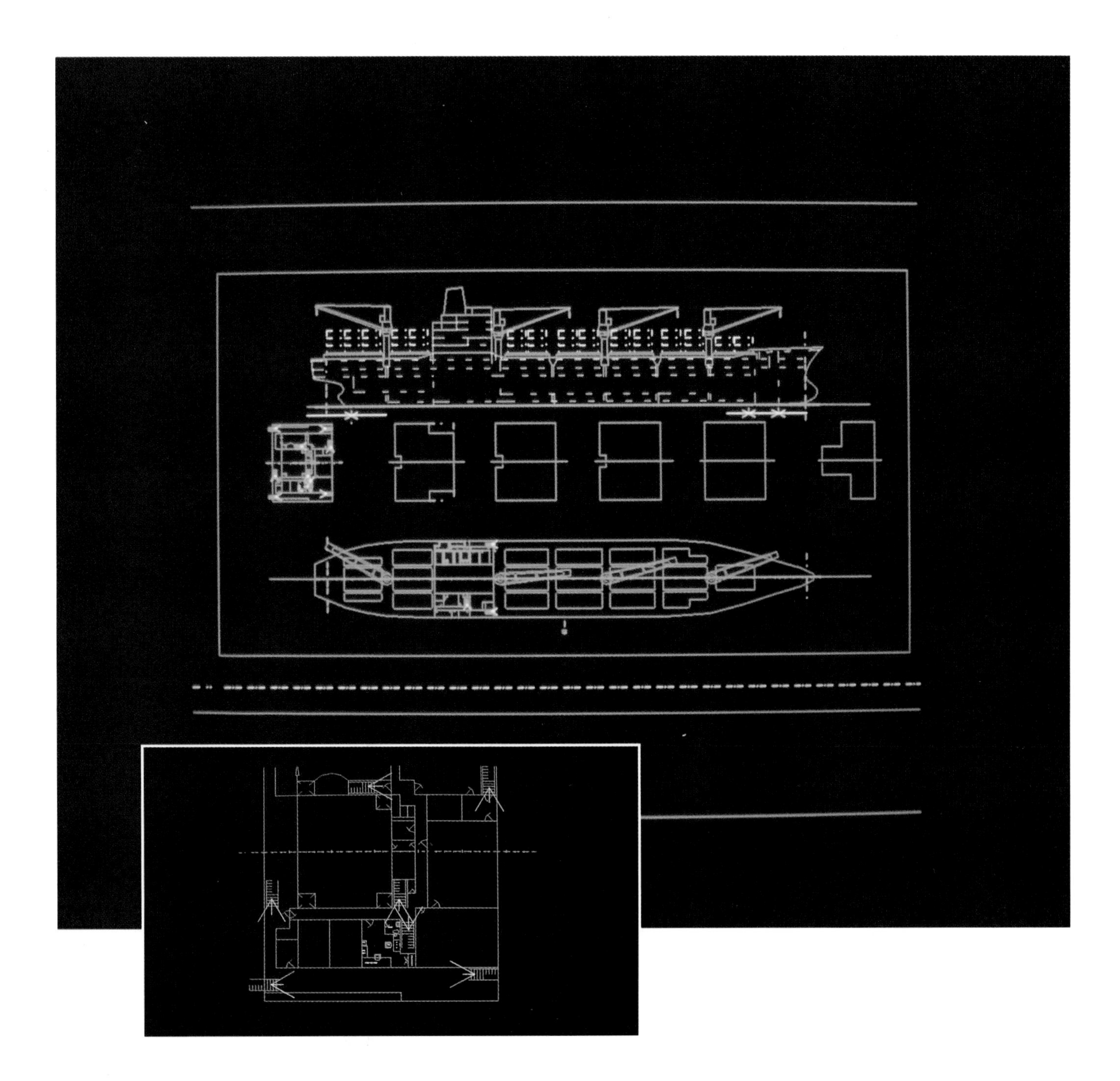

– such as whether the ship will have to negotiate the Panama Canal or the St Lawrence seaway.

Time-and-tide tables of intended areas of operation will be scrutinized to determine the ship's speeds, engine power and endurance. The type of cargo to be carried may well affect the design of equipment and of special features such as **derricks**. All these and many more aspects of the proposed ship will have to be established to ensure that the final design results in a vessel that is *safe, stable* and *seaworthy*.

When the naval architect's team has agreed upon the basic design, details are then submitted to the owners, confirming estimates of **displacement**, cargo or other carrying capacity, estimated horsepower of the engines, fuel consumption, and normal service speed.

If the design is based on other ships already in service or under construction the whole procedure is simplified, but for ships of a completely new design, tank-testing using scale models will have to be carried out.

Once the plans have been produced, the estimated cost of the project can be determined and the complete proposal submitted to the owner. If he accepts it, the building contract can be prepared and signed. The complex legal document specifies the design and technical data, the delivery date, the price and method of payment, and many other details.

When the formalities have been completed, hundreds of detailed drawings of all parts of the ship are prepared and distributed to the production departments.

Structural Stability

Once in a while you may read or hear of a ship "breaking her back" while laboring in a heavy sea, or through suffering structural damage in running aground, or perhaps in a collision.

The sea exerts immense pressures upon a ship's structure – especially if the ship is long and narrow. As the length of ships has extended more and more during the past few decades (particularly in the case of crude carriers, the largest of which is 1500 feet, or 458 meters, long) – so the danger of structural stress has increased quite considerably.

The three most common stress factors are **hogging**, **sagging** and **shearing**. If one or more of these factors is exerted on a ship with inadequate strength in her structure, her back will be broken. Similarly, a collision or grounding followed by pummelling from heavy seas could fracture the keel of a ship.

The keel is the lowest, continuous line of steel plates extending the whole length of a ship. Fixed to the keel are the stem, the **stern post**, and the ribs or **frames**. Together they form the ship's strongest single member. In most ships, two additional keels – known as **bilge keels** – are fitted to the hull on either side of the central keel to assist the ship's launch. They also help to minimize rolling in a heavy sea.

A vessel rolls because the water level is higher on one side than on the other: if these levels vary greatly and coincide with the ship's natural roll, the result can be quite violent. Rolling can be partially arrested by fitting **fin stabilizers**. Other special roll dampers or anti-rolling devices are fitted to ships, especially to those that carry passengers.

A naval architect must guard against all kinds of stresses when designing the structural stability of a ship.

Hogging Lengthwise, or longitudinal, strength is vital in order to withstand the stress that occurs when the midsection of a ship is supported by the crest of a wave.

Sagging When the bows and stern of a ship are supported by wave crests, the center section is left unsupported. It can lead to a vessel breaking up amidships and sinking.

Shearing As the lengths of ships increase, so the designer's problems multiply. Very long tankers and bulk carriers are especially susceptible to ocean and wave conditions that can produce the effect of being supported by three wave crests (as arrowed).

Below. Stabilizers act like fins on either side of the ship to modify the rolling motion. They are withdrawn into the hull of the ship when not at sea.

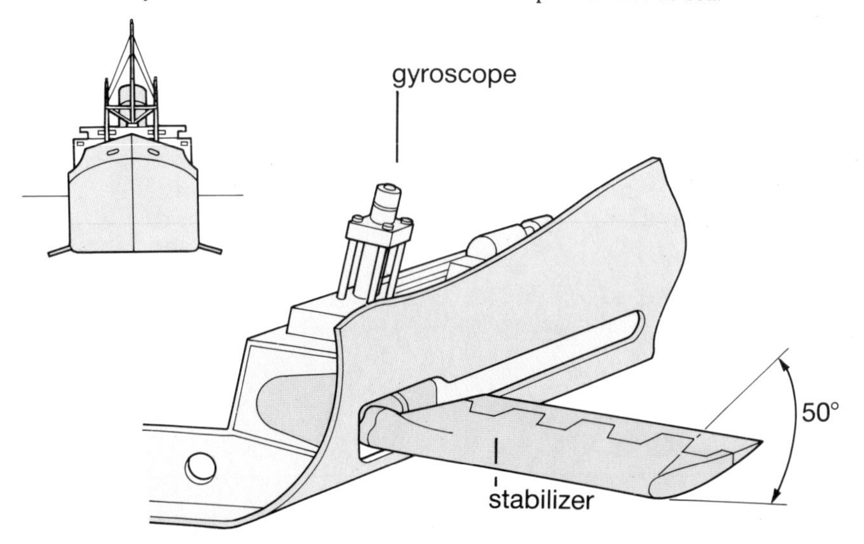

Model Tank Testing

A digital computer can produce a mass of design data, but for a ship that has specific functional requirements – such as a Liquified Natural Gas (LNG) carrier, a cruise ship or a barge carrier – or for an entirely new type of ship, a scale model must be constructed. This will then be put through a series of rigorous and carefully controlled tests in a special tank.

Models generally vary in size from 10 to 20 feet (3 to 6 meters) and are made of a malleable material such as wax. When in the test tank, their performance is electronically monitored. Various sea conditions are simulated and the model's resistance to them is measured. The resulting performance statistics are then computer analyzed. From the data, the scientists and designers are able to predict the ship's reaction to what are known as her "service conditions" – the seas in which she will serve.

Modifications to the wax model can be made by means of cutters or **scribing tools** guided by an electronic eye that can reshape the model to conform to the revised data. This monitoring device ensures accuracy to extremely fine tolerances.

The tests will confirm – or correct – the architect's calculations as to the required horsepower. They will tell him how to help conserve energy, how to increase the ship's speed, and how to lower her fuel consumption – vital information for the prospective owners, who want to operate their vessels at the lowest possible cost per unit ton of fuel or cargo. The tests will also point the way to improvements – for example, lessening a tendency to pitch into a head sea – and will ensure the maximum safety, strength and steadiness of the ship when she is at sea.

Model tank testing is a vital factor in the building of a ship. It is essential to resolve as many problems as possible at this stage, when the costs are relatively low.

Tank testing is carried out to assess the feasibility of ship design before construction begins. On the left, the model of a cargo vessel is being positioned in a tank to check handling and maneuverability. The picture above shows a hull model being tested for wave resistance and propulsion.

Construction Hall

The largest covered shipbuilding construction hall in the free world dominates the skyline of Barrow Island near Birkenhead in England. With its associated workshops and amenities it covers an area of 6.17 acres (25,000 sq. meters). Standing 167 feet (51 meters) high, it is tall enough for overhead cranes to clear the raised masts of a nuclear submarine or the superstructure to mid-mast level of a fleet destroyer.

Several radio-controlled overhead cranes, of up to 150 tons capacity, run on rails the length of the building. Workshops and stores are provided at each side of the hall on two levels. This ensures that all facilities are alongside the build-and-fitting-out positions.

Six amenity towers house locker rooms, mess rooms, conference rooms, showers and other facilities.

Ship units under construction in the hall are mounted on huge **cradles** and are transported on rails by highly powered **bogies** to the building line or other product areas.

A notable feature of this construction hall is the massive **ship elevator**, which is able to raise or lower uniformly distributed loads of up to 24,300 tons. It has the largest capacity of any elevator in the western world and is 531 feet (162 meters) long and has 54 beams. Each of the 108 electrical **winches** by which it is activated has a nominal lifting capacity of 225 tons. One of the ship elevator's first tasks was to lift the new diesel/electric submarine *Upholder* – a mere 2,400 tons!

These huge all-purpose construction halls are a feature of modern shipyards. Organization differs according to the vessel or the product. Typically, the hall will contain the **plate** preparation facility and the assembly shop, both of which are equipped with the most modern plate-forming and steel-handling equipment and automatic welding processes. Here groups of skilled workers in integrated teams work on large sections of a vessel as separate free-standing, pre-fitted-out units, which are then assembled with other large sections to form the completed vessel. This is sometimes known as *modular construction*.

Right. At 2,400 tons, the diesel-electric patrol submarine *Upholder* was a relatively small load for this powerful ship elevator, which is capable of raising loads ten times as heavy. In the background, the massive doors give an indication of the size of the Construction Hall, which can easily accommodate more than one ship at a time.

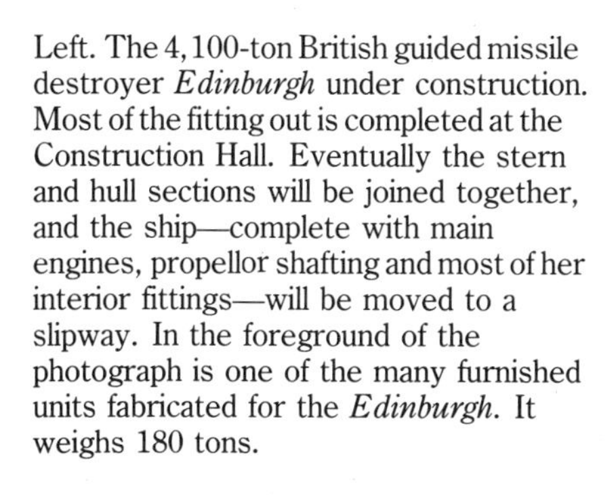

Left. The 4,100-ton British guided missile destroyer *Edinburgh* under construction. Most of the fitting out is completed at the Construction Hall. Eventually the stern and hull sections will be joined together, and the ship—complete with main engines, propellor shafting and most of her interior fittings—will be moved to a slipway. In the foreground of the photograph is one of the many furnished units fabricated for the *Edinburgh*. It weighs 180 tons.

After completion, a deckhead assembly is lowered into position on to the ship in the Construction Hall.

The *Royal Viking Sun* under construction in the Wärtsilä Marine shipyard in Finland. She is shown being towed from her construction site. (Note the ice on the water in the foreground.) 669 feet (204 meters) and 95 feet (29 meters) wide, she has a displacement of 38,000 tons. Four main engines give a speed of nearly 22 knots. She has been designed to carry over 1,150 passengers and 460 crew on cruises to the tropics.

Steel Preparation

Modern steel preparation techniques include computer-controlled robotic cutters, shown here under supervision by an operator. The robots work to fine tolerances which ensure great dimensional accuracy.

Before the steel plates and beams ("stiffeners" is the technical term) can be used, they have to be thoroughly prepared, cut to size, and shaped ready for further processing. During storage in the steel mills or the company's stockyard they will have become coated with a thin film of rust and **scale**; they may also have become a little distorted. These defects have to be remedied, as follows:

Levelling or Plate Straightening. When the plates are welded they must be dimensionally accurate, free from stress and without any sign of buckling. To correct any distortion, the plates are fed through a series of light and heavy straightening rollers, which also remove or relieve stresses.

Shotblasting. This is the name given to the process of firing fine abrasive particles and sometimes small metal shot at a metal surface. It removes all traces of rust and scale, and prepares the base metal to receive a primer paint that will prevent immediate re-rusting. The process is often carried out on a chain-conveyor system, which transports the plates, sections, rolled and fabricated profiles through the cleaning and priming plant.

Cutting. Modern oxyacetylene and oxypropane gas torches are used for cutting plates, complicated profiles, and internal cut outs (holes). This is controlled by electronic devices that read or scan a one-tenth scale drawing of the cutting profile. Thick plates can be cut by **flame planers**, two or three at a time; thin plates are simply guillotined.

Stiffeners, which are much stronger than plates, are usually flame-gas cut or sawn. The lighter ones are cropped in a guillotine before they are welded on to the plates.

Bending. The biggest and most important stiffeners are usually curved or bent to shape by heavy duty three-roll **frame benders** of enormous power which are computer controlled and hydraulically operated. The process is known as "cold-forming," as it is carried out without subjecting the metal to heat. In one type of shipyard, a press may handle plates up to 52.5 feet (16 meters) long. In another, the roll press can exert a pressing force of 3,000 tons.

Special Purpose Pressing. Plates that cannot be processed by modern techniques are handled separately by workers trained in special skills.

The paint area consists of enormous temperature-controlled cells that can accommodate sections even larger than the one illustrated. Special spraying techniques are used for applying anti-corrosion coatings to the fabrications.

Fabrication and Pre-fitting-out

Until fairly recently, most ships were built on **slipways** sited on wide riverbanks. The ship's keel was laid, the structure was framed, stiffened and plated, and there followed a lengthy period of fitting-out after the launch. All this work was subject to changing weather conditions.

Today, slipways are still used for ships displacing around 250,000 tons **DWT**, but above that weight, a shallow **dry dock** is used; below it, a covered hall may prove more economical.

Modern technological advances have made it possible to pre-fabricate parts of the basic structure and to pre-assemble many of the major fittings – thus saving time and money.

Fabrication is the welding together of finished plates and stiffeners. The smaller units, or sub-assemblies, may be as light as a ton. The larger units, or assemblies – also known as sections, blocks, modules, and weldments – may weigh as much as 500 tons. A sophisticated system of flow production, from preparation shop to fabrication shop, ensures that the sections, or blocks, are built in sequence and then welded or "faired" to each other to form larger units.

Pre-fitting-out is the preparing of the units before they are fitted to the ship's structure. For example, the cabins of a passenger liner – and there may be hundreds of them – can be constructed as modules. They are then painted and completely fitted out with doors, cupboards, cabinets, electrical and sanitary fixtures, etc., and lowered into the hull or sections of the hull. The same modular techniques are applied to massive structures such as **deckheads** and **deckhouses**.

To move and hoist the modules on to the main structure, self-elevating transporters and massive cranes with 840-ton capacity are used.

The bridge module has been built in a fabrication shop before being transported to the ship under construction. Here it is shown being lowered onto a passenger liner by cranes. The size of the module can be judged by the height of the men standing on the upper deck.

Modern techniques demand that as much pre-fitting-out as possible is done at an early stage of construction. This is often achieved by completing a number of modules—e.g. sets of cabins, crew's quarters and shops—then building them into the ship at her fitting-out berth. The high standards of design and workmanship can be seen in this photograph of a ship's beauty salon.

Engines and Machinery

One of the most exacting processes in the building of a ship is the installation of the main propulsion unit, the engine. But before that can happen – and while the engine itself is still under construction – marine engineers and other technicians have to carry out the installation and fitting-out work, much of it of an intricate nature.

For example, the electricians have to fit scores of auxiliary electrical and mechanical items – such as alternators, motors and pumps – all of which combine to complete the engine room installation. Also included are the wiring, pipework and valves. Like a house, a ship needs lighting, cooling, heating, ventilating and air-conditioning.

In addition to the "domestic" fixtures and fittings, the electricians have the responsibility of installing a whole range of highly technical apparatus and equipment – such as advanced navigational aids, radar, sonar and communications – which are now essential in even some of the smallest vessels.

Of equal importance is the work of the plumbers who, as well as installing the normal fittings like those used in your home, also look after the pumps and pipework for **ballast**, fuel oil, lubricating oil and, in the case of tankers, etc., internal transfer of liquid cargoes.

The Engine

The most common marine propulsion engine today is the direct-drive diesel, operating at around 115 to 120 revolutions per minute. Some of these immense engines weigh not far short of 2,000 tons.

A typical slow-speed, direct-drive diesel engine used in the recent past is the 2-stroke exhaust turbocharged crosshead. In this engine, fuel is burned on one side of the **piston** only.

Some of the sophisticated equipment in the Combat Information Center in a US submarine. Most ships nowadays are equipped with electronic navigational and communication aids; even fishing craft use sonar for the detection of schools of fish.

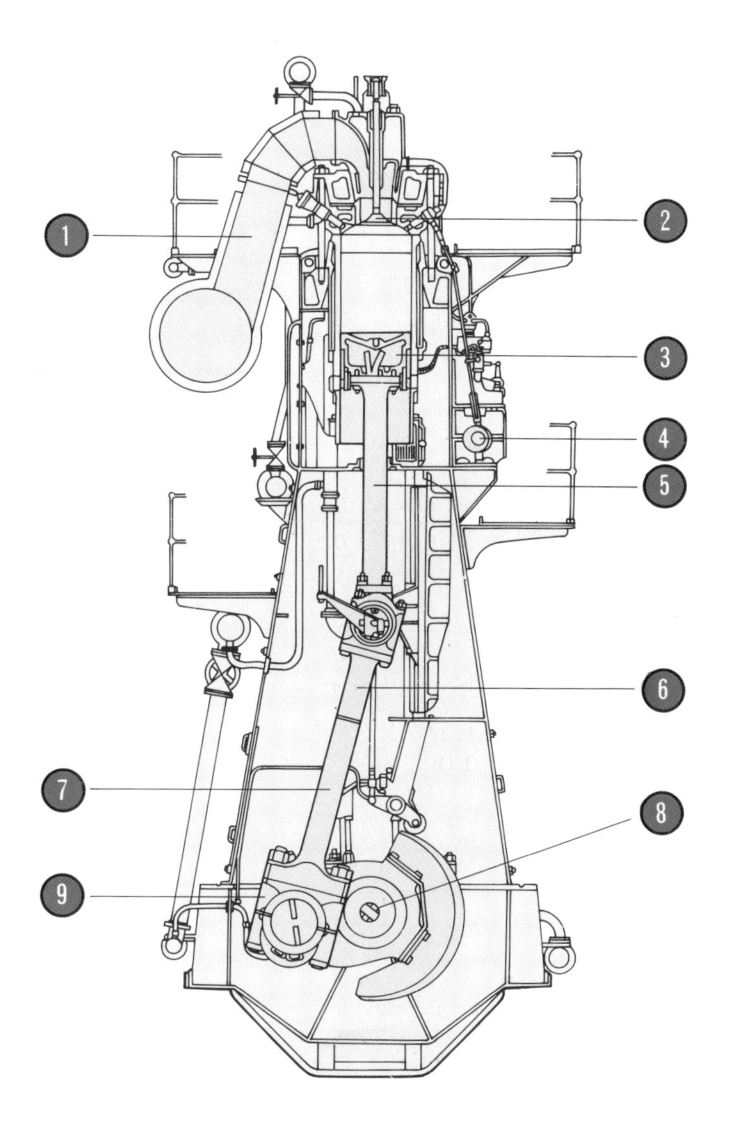

Typical of many marine propulsion engines in use throughout the world is the 2-stroke crosshead, direct drive propulsion diesel engine. The cross-section above shows its main components.

1. Exhaust pipe
2. Exhaust gas valve
3. Oil cooled working piston
4. Camshaft
5. Piston rod
6. Crosshead bearing
7. Connecting rod
8. Crank shaft
9. Crank end bearing

The **side thrust** of the piston rod is taken on a crosshead, which forces the rod into a simple up and down movement. This is known as a single-acting engine.

Nowadays turbocharging is invariably by blowers or by compression, the gas turbines being activated by the exhaust gases discharged through the cylinders. Such engines are built to enormous dimensions. A typical **cylinder bore** size is 41.3 inches (1.05 meters), which is more than ten times the size of an average family car engine. The stroke, at 70.8 inches (1.8 meters) is about twenty times the size of the car. Running at 105 rpm this engine develops about 4,000 HP.

The 12-cylinder version, known as a "cathedral" engine is nearly 85.3 feet (26 meters) long and up to 45.9 feet (14 meters) high.

Steam turbines, although popular, are gradually being displaced by diesels; in fact, some steam Very Large Crude Carriers are being re-engined with diesels.

Typical of the modern long-range container ship is the *Tolaga Bay.* With an engine of only two-thirds the horse power of those of her predecessors, she can transport twelve times as much cargo, and can steam an average of 5 knots faster.

The bridge of a merchant ship is fitted with all the electronic equipment required by the captain and his watch-keeping officers. As well as navigational aids, such as radar and a satellite navigation system, the equipment includes an auto pilot for steering the ship, direct engine controls, and a number of computer consoles that activate machinery operated by remote control.

Left. The launching of the 44,000 ton liner *Canberra*. Once off the slipway, her progress through the water was slowed down by drag chains connecting her to the shore until tugs could be positioned to maneuver her into the fitting-out berth. Floating in the water on either side are the cradles that supported her as she slid down the slipway.

Right. As an engineering feat, the floating-out method is far less spectacular than a slipway launch, but the early morning float-out of this large vessel from the Building Dock has a dramatic visual impact.

Launching

One of the most spectacular events in a shipyard is the launching of a vessel from an **inclined berth**. Despite the introduction of other more modern systems – such as **floating out** from a building dock – the inclined slipway is still the most popular method of launching.

A launch is by no means the deceptively simple, smooth-running operation that it may appear to be. The days leading up to it are fraught with anxiety for all shipyard officials and for the naval architect and his team, who in addition to designing the ship are responsible for the launching calculations.

Things do not always go as planned. For example, a ship once turned turtle on taking to the water, and on many occasions vessels have failed to move down the slipway into the water.

The most celebrated set-back was during the launching of Brunel's *Great Eastern* in 1858. The world's largest ship of her time was moving off *sideways* from her berth on the River Thames when she came to a halt, couldn't be budged, and remained there for months. Her builders went out of business, and the nerve-wracking experience contributed to Brunel's early death.

Even before the very early stages of construction it is customary to make preliminary calculations for the launch. Keel blocks are laid along a centerline and the ship is built on these.

Just before the launch, the final calculations are checked, the weight and center of gravity of the ship are estimated, and **tide tables** are studied to determine the height and the tide most suitable for the launch.

The science of moving a newly-built ship from dock to water consists primarily of transferring the ship's weight from her keel blocks and **shores** (which have supported her during construction) to fixed **launchways**. Then both the ship and the **sliding ways** are allowed to slip down the launchways into the water. A thin layer of grease is applied to the top surfaces of the launchways to separate them from the sliding ways.

Timber wedges and filling pieces (known as "daggers" and "triggers") are placed on top of the sliding ways and "made up" to the underside of the hull, so that when the wedges are hammered home the whole weight of the ship will be firmly transferred from the keel or building blocks to the launchways.

The workmen begin at the water's edge, following a carefully planned schedule, so that an hour or so before the actual launching ceremony the ship is standing high on her launchways, held in position by the wedges and filling pieces.

The site is cleared; the propellor and the rudder are locked; the ship's manager, pilot and deck crew go aboard; the **tugs** take up station; and the naming ceremony begins. When the formalities are completed, the wedges are released and the ship takes over, gradually gathers momentum, and then plunges stern first into the water. It is a carefully controlled, not a headlong, plunge, as the speed is being arrested by fixed **drag chains**, which act like a brake.

Nowadays another method of launching is used which is less spectacular but has direct links with the past. Centuries ago on the banks of the River Thames it was usual to construct dry docks by digging small inlets and damming them. In these berths wooden ships were built, and to launch them the dam wall was removed, resulting in a float-out.

In 1844 Brunel adopted this principle in Bristol by using a cemented dry dock for his *Great Britain*. The ship is now still to be seen in the same dock.

The modern method of float out is more complicated, but the principle is the same. The ship is constructed out of doors in a dry dock served by massive cranes and sealed by an enormous floating **caisson** (pronounced *cassoon*). When ready for launch the ship is simply floated out by opening the caisson and flooding the dock.

Some Ultra Large Crude Carriers are now so enormous that no dry dock is big enough to accommodate them. They are therefore constructed in two halves. Each half is launched separately and floated out to a berth, and then the two halves are joined together.

Fitting-out

Though a good deal of pre-fitting-out of modules is carried out in the construction hall, much of the extra finishing work is completed while the ship is secured alongside in the fitting-out basin. This work is known as fitting-out.

The propellor and rudder are fitted to the hull during the construction stage, but certain other bulky items of machinery are not installed until later. These may include the main engine and boilers.

The type and extent of fitting will obviously depend on the ship: for example, a tanker will need less work than a liner. In the case of a luxury liner, fitting-out would consist of putting on all the finishing touches – furnishings, upholstery, carpeting, curtaining, etc. – to the passenger cabins, offices, lounges, stores, restaurants and other public rooms.

Meanwhile, on deck, the lifeboats are fitted on to their **davits**. Safety regulations require that there must be enough lifeboats to accommodate all the ship's crew and passengers. The boats are securely stowed, high up on the upper decks, to protect them from rough seas. Other safety and firefighting gear also has to be installed. Finally comes the major task of cleaning and painting the whole ship before she leaves the fitting-out berth. For a passenger liner this is time-consuming enough. For a supertanker and her acres of steelwork – including the extensive piping systems located on the main deck – it is a mammoth operation, taking up to several weeks before the vessel can officially be declared ready for final acceptance.

The variation in fitting-out requirements of different types of ship are clearly illustrated in these pictures. The ferry fitting out in a Finnish shipyard (below left) requires considerable work on passenger accommodation, whereas in the tanker astern of her the emphasis is on complicated pipework and monitoring controls to ensure that the tanks are gas-free. In contrast, the electrical and electronic complexities of radar and communication systems on a French aircraft carrier (right) put the emphasis on technological fitting-out.

The luxurious styling of the *Royal Princess* cruise liner (below) calls for specialist designer work. The elegant finishes and high quality materials make the fitting-out very costly.

Testing and Sea Trials

The more sophisticated the design and construction of a ship, the more complicated the testing procedures and the trials that she has to undergo. For example, computer-controlled communication and navigation systems have to be tested and checked at almost every stage of installation, as well as after launching.

Even the most solid structures, such as the basic steelwork, are systematically checked for flaws. Metal that has been welded is carefully inspected by means of **radiography**, and in some areas laser equipment is used to ensure total accuracy.

When fitting-out is completed, other important tests are carried out. Compartments, tanks and compressors are subjected to **liquid pressure testing** and they have to be certified as conforming to specified standards.

All cargo-handling equipment is tested to a maximum loading point. Each item of electrical equipment is checked. All plumbing services are inspected to the satisfaction of marine surveyors and inspectors, and the safety of the ship and the crew is always uppermost in their minds.

During the weeks following fitting out of the ship, a series of sea trials are held. Again, safety is the most important factor and the first trials are devoted to checking major items of equipment such as the anchor and the windlass. Adjustments must be made to the ship's compass, correcting any inaccuracy caused by the magnetic effect of the steel structure. To check vibration, the engines are run at different speeds, including full astern.

To test the steering gear the ship is put through a series of rigorous maneuvers, such as an emergency stop, similar to that in a motorist's driving test. The larger the ship, the more difficult it is to stop: for example, during her trials the 480,000 DWT *Globtik Tokyo* went a distance of 2.75 miles from full ahead to dead in the water.

A series of tests at different engine powers are carried out over a measured mile: the new ship being timed at least once in each direction past permanently sited shore markers. These tests are known as "progressive speed trials."

Many other tests are conducted by representatives from the outside contractors, like navigational and communication specialists.

After completing a series of rigorous tests and trials, a completed vessel is accepted by a representative of the ship owners. Here the MV *Patricia* is seen on her final acceptance trials.

Design for the 21st Century

A major current project for the Royal Navy, the *Landing Platform Dock* (LPD) is designed as a headquarters ship for an amphibious fleet that can transport men and vehicles efficiently and quickly. Specially adapted for use in unpleasant sea conditions – such as very high winds and icy waters – she has what is known as a "high degree of survivability" and a "built-in stability," which means that she will be difficult to destroy or sink. She will be equipped with *Electronic Counter Measures* (ECM) for self-defense, and a *Close-In Weapons System* (CIWS) for an offensive (anti-aircraft) role. She will also have a fully integrated Command, Control and Communications System.

The United States Navy is planning a new warship which will virtually be "invisible" to radar, surveillance systems, spy satellites, and other detection devices, both in space and at sea. It is believed that such a ship – a surface vessel with most of the best qualities of a submarine – could ensure command of the seas for decades to come. It is envisaged that she will have a smooth, rounded profile, probably constructed from **composites**, including graphite. Cooling equipment will counter heat-sensing missiles or detection devices by reducing **infra-red emissions** from the engine and exhausts.

Another ship of the future is the Single Well Oil Production and Storage Ship (SWOPS) now under development at the Harland and Wolff shipyard in Belfast, Northern Ireland. Designed to service "marginal" oil wells – those too small and too uneconomical for permanent rigs but producing sizeable volumes of oil from depths down to over 650 feet (200 meters) – the SWOPS will in effect be a mobile rig, storage tanker, and processing plant all in one. The oil will be extracted, processed, and pumped into storage tanks. When fully loaded the ship will transport her cargo to a shore depot.

This fascinating new vessel will have a displacement of 76,000 tons, an overall length of 825.1 feet (251.5 meters) and an oil storage capacity of 51,000 tons. Seven computer-controlled motorized **thrusters** – like those in space satellites – will provide her with pinpoint accuracy in holding her position over the wells without the need for anchoring.

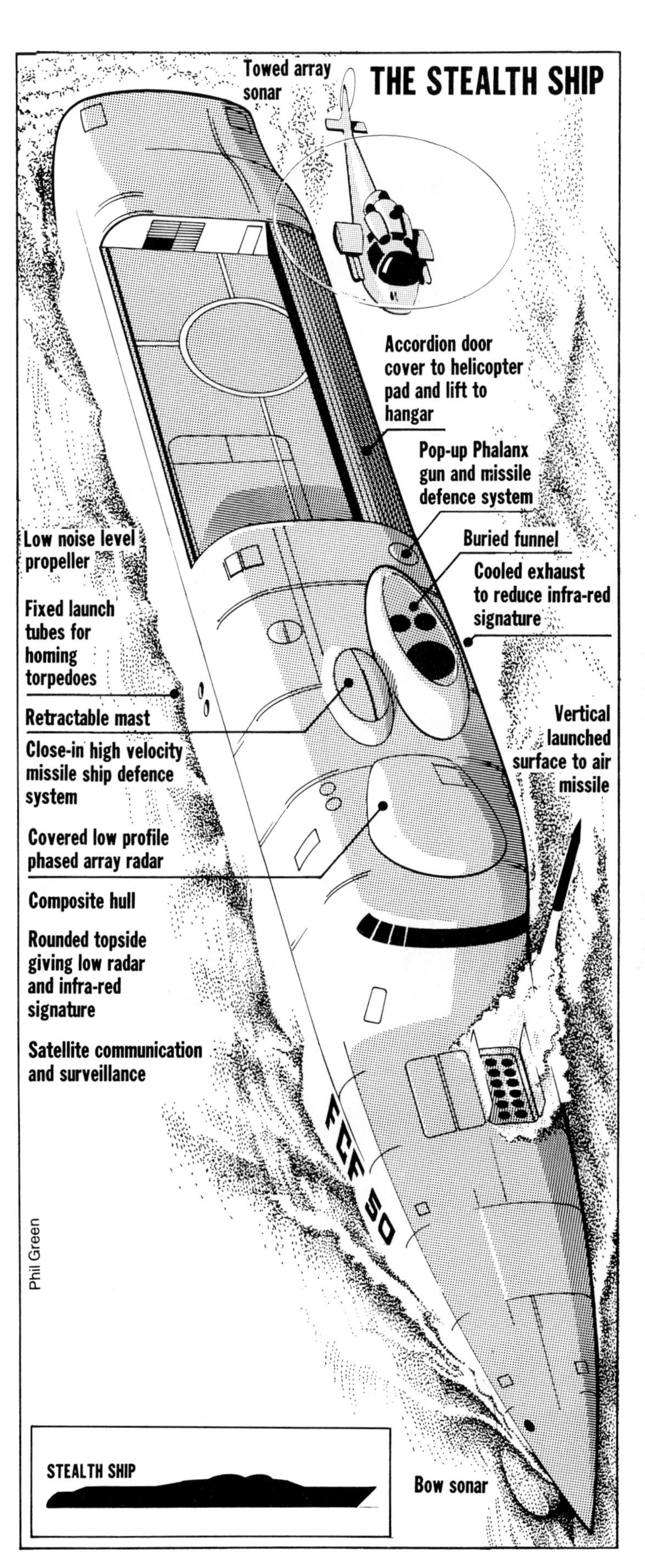

It is thought that the "invisibility" of the Stealth ship will revolutionize the future deployment of maritime forces.

Right. Landing Platform Dock vessels (LPD) are HQ ships for amphibious forces. By flooding compartments in the ship, as in a dock, landing craft can be floated out through the open stern. The latest design provides rapid and efficient deployment of a military force of tanks, motor vehicles and men.

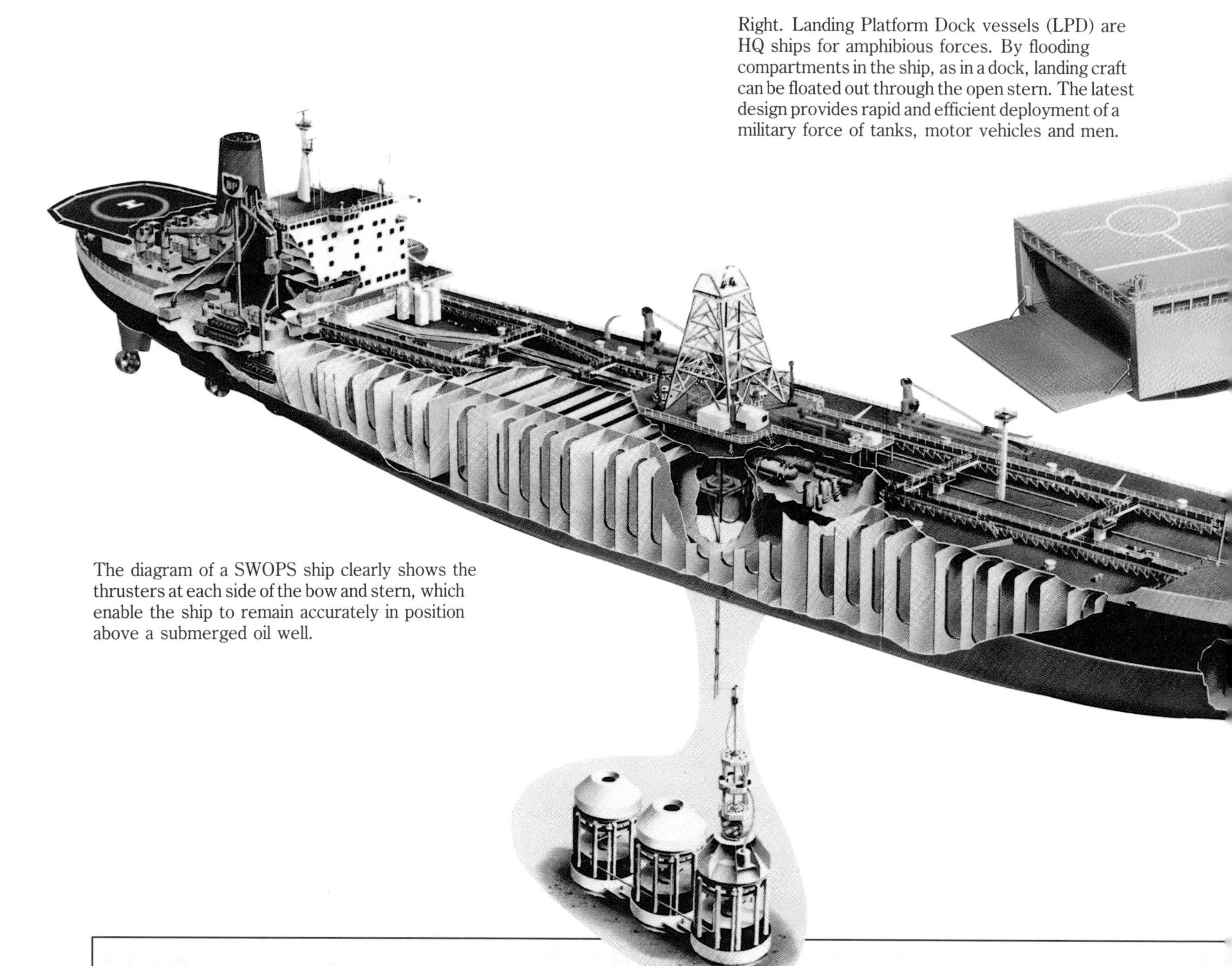

The diagram of a SWOPS ship clearly shows the thrusters at each side of the bow and stern, which enable the ship to remain accurately in position above a submerged oil well.

IMPORTANT DATES

c1500 BC Ancient Egyptians built oared ships.
c1000 BC Ships with sails and banks of rowers introduced.
c800 BC Ships built with double decks.
c260 BC Romans built fleet of ships for Mediterranean conquest.
c896 AD King Alfred built a fleet of ships propelled by oars and sails.
1209-12 King John built fifty new ships for England's Navy.
1260 Guild of Free Shipwrights formed in London.
1340 King Edward III built a navy which earned him the name 'King of the Seas'.
c1485 King Henry VII laid foundation of the Royal Navy.
1502 Mariner's compass invented by the Italian Flavio Gioja, resulting in increased shipbuilding.
1509-47 King Henry VIII built a large fleet of ships – among them the enormous *Henry Grâce à Dieu*. He also set up the Admiralty and several dockyards.
1583 First attempt at steam propulsion by Blasco de Garay in Barcelona, Spain, using a cauldron of boiling water.
1769 First efficient steam engine patented in England by James Watt.
1801 *Charlotte Dundas*, the first successful paddle steamer, built in England by W. Symington, with an engine by James Watt.
1807 First regular run by paddle steamer *Clermont*, built in the USA by Robert Fulton, the Irish-American designer.
1810-20 Robert Leppings, surveyor to the British Navy, advanced the science of shipbuilding by introducing a new method of hull construction.
1832 First Baltimore clipper, the *Ann McKim*, designed and built by Donald McKay.
1839 *Archimedes*, designed by Pettit Smith, the first steamer powered by a single screw propellor.
1843 I.K. Brunel launched the huge revolutionary ship *Great Britain*, 3,270 tons.
1855 *Lloyd's Register of Shipping* published first rules for iron shipbuilding and in 1857 for steel-built ships.
1858 *Great Eastern* launched in England. She was three times the size of any ship ever built, and carried 4,000 passengers.
1860 HMS *Warrior*, 9,210 tons, the first all-iron warship.
1873 HMS *Devastation*, the first sea-going ship without sails or rigging. 9,330 tons, and 4 – 12 inch guns.

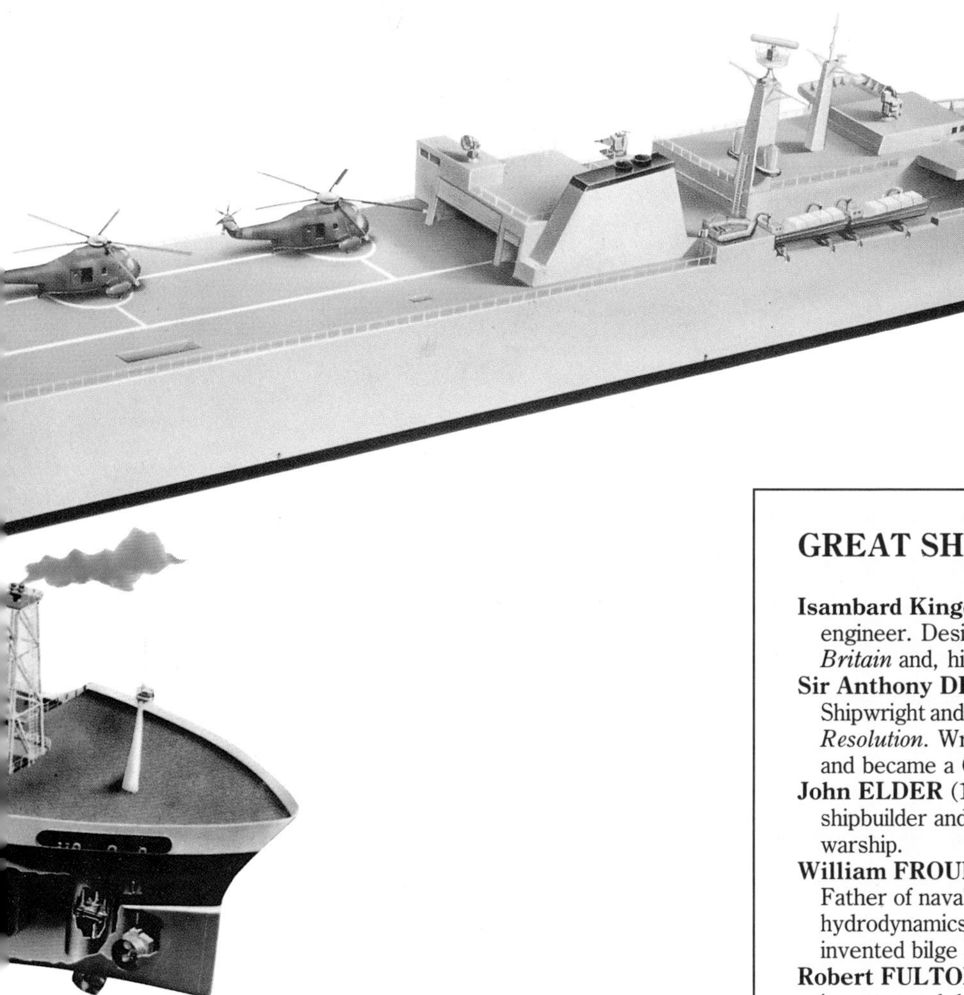

1894	World's first turbine vessel, the *Turbinia,* built in Newcastle, England.
1903	First diesel and electric ship, the *Wandel,* built in England.
1906	HMS *Dreadnought,* battlecruiser, built in a year and a day.
1912	The first ocean-going motor ship, *Selandia,* launched in Denmark.
1939-45	World War II: precipitated tremendous increases in shipbuilding activity: e.g. in the US Henry Kaiser built 2,270 'Liberty' ships; the Royal Navy grew to 3,500 ships including 57 carriers; the German navy commissioned over 1,000 submarines.
1954	USS *Nautilus,* world's first nuclear-powered submarine, commissioned.
1961	World's first nuclear-powered ballistic missile submarine joined the US Navy.
1972	First plastic (GRP = glass reinforced plastic) warship launched, the minesweeper HMS *Wilton.*
1975	First of the 'Nimitz' class of nuclear-powered aircraft carriers launched in the USA. She is still the largest warship in the world.

GREAT SHIP DESIGNERS

Isambard Kingdom BRUNEL (1806-1859). English engineer. Designed and built the *Great Western,* the *Great Britain* and, his greatest achievement, the *Great Eastern.*

Sir Anthony DEANE (c1638-1721). English Master Shipwright and Admiral. Designed and built the *Rupert* and *Resolution.* Wrote *The Doctrine of Naval Architecture* and became a Commissioner of the Navy.

John ELDER (1824-1869). English ship designer, shipbuilder and marine engineer. Patented a circular warship.

William FROUDE (1810-1879). Born in Devon, England. Father of naval architecture. Pioneered the science of hydrodynamics – using scale models in water tanks – and invented bilge keels to reduce rolling in ships.

Robert FULTON (1765-1815). American engineer, inventor and designer of the *Clermont.* Built a submarine in 1800.

Donald McKAY (1810-1880). American designer of the famous Baltimore clippers. Built the *Lightning,* one of the fastest sailing ships in the world, as well as the *Champion of the Seas* and the *James Baines.*

Robert NAPIER (1791-1876). British marine engineer. Designed and supplied hundreds of marine engines. Also designed more than 300 vessels.

Sir Charles PARSONS (1854-1931). British engineer. Invented the steam turbine for marine propulsion. In 1894 designed and built the torpedo boat *Turbinia,* the first to be fitted with turbine engines.

Phineas PETT (1570-1647). With his son, Peter, designed and built the *Sovereign of the Seas.* This English family produced at least ten master shipwrights between 1560 and 1660.

John Scott RUSSELL (1808-1882). Scottish naval architect and civil engineer. Built Brunel's *Great Eastern* and was joint designer of the *Warrior* and of many other ships.

Admiral David Watson TAYLOR, USN (1864-1940). American naval constructor and designer of ships and of naval aircraft. Supervised US Navy building program in World War I.

Sir John Isaac THORNYCROFT (1843-1928). British pioneer of naval architecture. Designer of high speed ships, torpedo boats and racing motor boats.

George Lennox WATSON (1851-1904). Scottish naval architect. Over a period of thirty years designed passenger and cargo ships, but famous for his design of hundreds of yachts, including the 'J' class cutter *Britannia* owned by King George V.

William Henry WEBB (1816-1899). American shipbuilder. Ranked high as a designer of clippers. Also designed and built steamships, warships and an ironclad.

Sir William Henry WHITE (1845-1913). English naval architect. Director of Naval Construction at the Admiralty. Designed more than 40 battleships and over 30 cruisers.

Glossary

Ballast Heavy material, such as pig iron or water, stored in the bottom of the ship to keep her steady. Modern ships have ballast tanks built into them. When a ship has discharged her cargo and sails empty she is ballasted by flooding water into her ballast tanks to give her stability.
Berth Usually refers to the quay or jetty alongside which a ship lies for loading and unloading cargo. A building berth is the inclined or sloping slipway on which a ship is built and from which she is launched.
Bilge keel Lengthwise keel secured to the hull on either side of the main keel to provide stability.
Bogie An undercarriage used for transporting.
CAD/CAM Computer Assisted (or Aided) Design/ Computer Assisted Manufacture. These are computer programs to assist the Naval Architect and the shipbuilders in designing and building the ship.
Caisson A dock gate which floats and can be positioned at the dock entrance by sinking it into position. Caissons are used in dry docks and non-tidal basins to prevent the water getting into a dry dock or to stop it from getting out of a non-tidal basin when the tide goes out.
Centerline An imaginary line drawn from the bow to the stern post, dividing the ship in half.
Cladding Plates of iron which are clad or secured to the hull of a wooden ship to give it protection.
Class Collective name for ships of similar size and design.
Clipper The fast ocean-going sailing ships originating in Baltimore in the early 19th century. Such ships, owned by companies in America and Great Britain, used to compete with one another in the tea trade with China and India.
Composites Building materials of different types. A boat or ship is said to be "composite-built" when the frames or ribs are of steel and the hull planking is of wood.
Containers The standard ISO-sized containers have modules 10, 20, 30 and 40 feet long. By far the most popular size is 8ft × 8.5ft × 20ft (2435mm × 2590mm × 6055mm).
Cradle Framework shaped to the curvature of the hull, which supports the ship on dry land. Cradles are fitted between the hull of the ship and the launching slipway to keep the hull upright. When the ship is launched, the cradles travel down the slipway with the ship.
Cylinder A circular chamber or hole within an engine which contains the piston.
Cylinder bore The diameter of the piston cylinder in which the piston operates. (See *Piston.*)
Davit An appliance designed for hoisting and lowering boats over the side of a ship.
Deckhead The nautical term for the ceiling of a compartment.
Deckhouse The structure fitted to the upper deck of a ship.
Derrick A large spar rigged as a boom to the mast of a ship and used for hoisting cargoes in and out of ships.
Displacement The amount of water which the hull of a ship displaces in the water (as in Archimedes' principle). This displacement is measured in tons. The displacement tonnage of a ship can vary, depending on whether she is fully loaded with cargo, or empty.
Drag chains Chains which are secured at one end to the land and at the other end to the hull of a ship before launching. They are used to slow and stop the ship when she enters the water from an inclined launching berth. Drag chains are used in narrow rivers or confined waters.
Dredger Vessel used in channels, harbors and rivers for deepening the water by excavation of the bed.
Dry dock A dock where the water is pumped out and in which a ship can be built or repaired. When the work is completed the dock is flooded with water and the ship floated out.
DWT Deadweight tonnage is the weight of cargo which a ship carries: plus the weight of fuel, stores, water ballast, fresh water, crew, passengers and baggage.
Flame planer A machine using a gas torch type flame to cut several steel plates at the same time.
Floating out Method of launching a ship after she has been built or fitted out in a dry dock by flooding the dock and floating her out.
Frame The term given to the ribs of a ship which are shaped to the hull and run from the keel to the upper deck.
Frame bender The machine which shapes the frames or ribs of the ship.
Galley A large vessel powered by oarsmen. Such craft were often fitted with sails.
Hogging Occurs when the bow and stern drop below an imaginary line between them.
Infra-red emissions Electro-magnetic radiation waves produced by machinery in ships and aircraft. The wavelengths of infra-red emissions can only be detected by special receivers.
Knot The measurement of the speed of a ship. One knot is one nautical mile per hour. A nautical mile is longer than a land mile. (See *Nautical mile.*)
Launchways (or launching ways, slipways or just "ways"). Wide, wooden slideways on which the cradles supporting a ship rest. Before the ship is launched, the launchways are heavily greased so that the cradles can move easily over them.
Liquid pressure testing When a tank or pressure vessel is constructed it is given a liquid pressure test to ensure that it does not leak.
Lloyd's Register of Shipping An 18th-century society founded in London, England to define rules regarding the construction of merchant ships.
LNG ship/tanker Vessels specially constructed to carry liquid natural gas. Natural gas is frozen

to a very low temperature of minus 163°C which makes the gas liquid. The liquid gas is then pumped into the LNG tanker which has highly insulated tanks to prevent the gas from evaporating.

LPG ship/tanker The construction of liquid petroleum gas-ships is similar to that of the LNG tankers. Propane or butane gases are frozen to make them liquid and then pumped into LPG tankers.

Nautical mile The length of a nautical mile is 2026 yards (1852 meters). A land mile is shorter: 1760 yards. (See *Knot.*)

OBO A combination bulk carrier which can transport oil, bulk or ore.

Panamax The largest size of vessel able to go through the Panama Canal.

Piston A solid cylinder which fits into the engine cylinder. The piston is connected to the crank shaft of the engine by a piston rod. Liquid or gas can be injected into the cylinder under pressure, which forces the piston to move within the cylinder. (See *Cylinder.*)

Plate or **plating** Sheets of steel used for building the hull of a ship.

Radiography (or X-ray) The method used for checking that a weld joining two steel plates together has been properly carried out. The X-ray shows up faulty welding or cracks in the weld.

Roll (or rolling). The side-to-side movement of the ship from the upright position. Rolling is caused by the motion of the sea on the ship.

Sagging The bow and the stern are above an imaginary line which joins them so that the keel has dropped.

Scale Loose surface of steel created by rust and heat treatment. Also a chemical deposit in a boiler.

Scantlings The dimensions of all parts of a ship's hull, including her frames, girders, stringers, plates, etc.

Screw A term used for the propellor of a ship. It is derived from the screw motion of the propellor through the water.

Scribe, to To engrave lines on steel plates by using sharp, pointed tools.

Sensor Device (such as sonar or radar) used to increase the senses of hearing and sight.

Shearing The hull is distorted about the center line or fore and aft line between the bow and stern. This distortion causes the ship to shear off a straight course.

Ship elevator A very large platform on which a ship sits and is then lifted out of the water so that work can be carried out under the water line.

Shore Large pieces of timber which support a vessel in the upright position in dry dock or on a slipway. When a ship dry-docks, shores are placed on each side, between the ship and the dock, while the water is being pumped out. More shores are fitted under the bottom of the ship to support her when the dock is emptied.

Side-thrust The sideways movement of a ship through the water when the bow or stern thrusters are used. (See *Thrusters.*)

Sonar A sonar-set in a ship can locate submarines under the water by transmitting sound waves towards the submarine. The sound waves bounce back off the submarine to a receiver in the ship. Computers work out the range, speed and depth of the submarine from the sound waves. The sonar principle is also used for measuring the depth of the water, to locate shoals of fish, and wrecks.

Stabilizers Moveable fins fitted in the ship's hull below the water line, which when operated help to decrease rolling. When not required, the fins are housed inside the hull, and when they are operated they are moved out into the water. The fins are operated by machinery in relation to a gyro in the stabilizer system, endeavoring to bring the ship back to an upright position.

Stern post A vertical piece of metal which supports the stern of a ship. It is located in the center of the stern in line with the keel.

Straightening roller Large rollers which straighten out steel plates and frames.

TEU Twenty-feet Equivalent Units: equivalent to 20ft containers.

Thrusters Propellors fitted in tunnels in the hull of a ship, at right angles to the center-line. They are usually fitted near the bow to assist in moving the ship sideways while at rest. Some ships which have to be accurately positioned have stern as well as bow thrusters.

Tide Tables or **Time-and-Tide Tables** Official publication listing times of the high and low water levels of tides throughout the world.

Tug Vessels designed to tow (pull) and push ships. Ocean-going tugs are used to help ships in distress at sea, or for towing ships, oil rigs and floating docks over a long distance. Harbor tugs are smaller and are used for berthing large ships, by pushing and pulling them into position.

Turbine engine A turbine is a wheel which is fitted with a large number of angled fins or blades instead of spokes. It is rotated by forcing high pressure steam or hot gases through the blades. A shaft running through the center of the turbine rotates, providing power. The power reaches the propellor shaft and the propellor through a gearbox. Turbine engines are usually fitted in fast warships and in some liners.

U-boat The Anglicized abbreviation of *Unterseeboot,* the German word for a submarine.

ULCC Ultra Large Crude Carrier.

VLCC Very Large Crude Carrier.

Winch An engine-driven drum used for hauling and hoisting.

Index

Acknowledgments

Threshold Books are grateful to the following for their assistance in compiling this book: Cammell Laird Shipbuilders Ltd, Birkenhead; Harland and Wolff Ltd, Belfast; Marine Design Consultants, Sunderland; Pegasus Ocean Services Ltd, London; Commander Ian Primrose; Swan Hunter Ltd, Walsend-on-Tyne, Michael J. Vincent, VSEL (Vickers Shipbuilding & Engineering) Ltd, Barrow-in-Furness.

Illustration credits
Photographs: British Marine Technology 13; Cammell Laird Shipbuilders Ltd front cover, 8, 14, 16 (top), 17; *Cutty Sark* Society 7 (top); Harland & Wolff Ltd 18, 23; by courtesy of IBM UK Ltd 10, 11; Mansell Collection 7 (bottom); National Maritime Museum 6; Popperfoto 24, 26; P & O Cruises Ltd 22, 25 (bottom); Spectrum Colour Library 3 (bottom); Frank Spooner Pictures/copyright GAMMA 2, 3 (center), 4, 5, 20, 25 (top); VSEL 9, 15, 29; Wärtsilä Marine 3 (top), 16 (bottom), 19, 21.

Drawings and diagrams: Phil Green/copyright Sunday Times, London 27; John Hutchinson 12, 21.

How Ships Are Made

Facts On File, Inc.
460 Park Avenue South
New York NY 10016
USA

Library of Congress Cataloging-in-Publication Data

Thomas, David Arthur, 1925–
 How ships are made/text, David A. Thomas; design, Eddie Poulton.
 32 p. 30 × 21 cm. (How it is made).
 Includes index.
 ISBN 0-8160-2040-X.
 1. Shipbuilding—Juvenile literature. 2. Naval architecture—Juvenile literature. [1. Discusses the history of shipbuilding and explains how modern ships are built from design through construction to testing and sea trials. 2. Shipbuilding. 3. Naval architecture.] I. Poulton, Eddie. II. Title. III. Series.
VM150.T46 1989
623.8′2—dc20 89-31328 CIP AC

Facts On File books are available at special discounts when purchased in bulk quantities for businesses, associations, institutions or sales promotion. Please contact the Special Sales Department of our New York office at 212/683-2244 (dial 800/322-8755 except in NY, AK or HI).

General Editor: Barbara Cooper.
Design by Eddie Poulton.
Composition by Rapid Communications Ltd, London, England.
Printed in England by Maclehose & Partners, Portsmouth.

10 9 8 7 6 5 4 3 2 1